2093

O9-AHW-119

Yellow Umbrella Books are published by Capstone Press
151 Good Counsel Drive, P.O. Box 669, Mankato, Minnesota 56002
http://www.capstone-press.com

Library of Congress Cataloging-in-Publication Data
Trumbauer, Lisa, 1963–
   Food for thought/by Lisa Trumbauer.
   p. cm.
   Includes index.
   ISBN 0-7368-0729-2
   1. Nutrition—Juvenile literature. [1. Nutrition. 2. Food.] I. Title.
TX355 .T73   2001
613.2—dc21   00-036805

   Summary: Describes the food pyramid, the various foods in each food group, and how the
   foods keep people healthy.

Editorial Credits:
Susan Evento, Managing Editor/Product Development; Elizabeth Jaffe, Senior Editor; Charles Hunt,
   Designer; Kimberly Danger and Heidi Schoof, Photo Researchers

Photo Credits:
Cover: Index Stock Imagery; Title page: (top to bottom) Bob Daemmrich/Pictor, Barbara
Peacock/FPG International LLC, Mike Malyszko/FPG International LLC, Visuals Unlimited/Robert
Clay; Page 2: Marilyn Moseley LaMantia (top left), Mike Malyszko/FPG International LLC (top
right), Photo Network/Esbin-Anderson (bottom); Page 4: Unicorn Stock Photos/Aneal Vohra (top
left), Unicorn Stock Photos/Jim Riddle (top right), Unicorn Stock Photos/Doug Adams (bottom left),
Unicorn Stock Photos/Martin Jones (bottom right); Page 5: Unicorn Stock Photos/Jeff Greenberg,
Visuals Unlimited/Erwin "Bud" Nielsen (inset); Page 6: Telegraph Colour Library/FPG International
LLC (top left), Unicorn Stock Photos/Robin Rudd (top right), Unicorn Stock Photos/Jim Shippee
(bottom left), Visuals Unlimited/M. Long (bottom right); Page 7: Craig D. Wood (left), Ken
Chernus/FPG International LLC (right); Page 8: Visuals Unlimited/Erwin "Bud" Nielsen (top left),
Unicorn Stock Photos/Tom McCarthy (top right), Photo Network/Henryk T. Kaiser (middle left),
Visuals Unlimited/D.S. Kerr (middle right), Unicorn Stock Photos/Eric Berndt (bottom left), Photo
Network/Esbin-Anderson (bottom right); Page 9: David F. Clobes, Visuals Unlimited/Arthur Hill
(inset); Page 10: Visuals Unlimited/Wally Eberhart (top left), Visuals Unlimited/E. Webber (top
middle), Visuals Unlimited/Valorie Hodgson (top right), Visuals Unlimited/Patricia Drentea (bottom
left), Photo Network/Jeff Greenberg (bottom middle), Visuals Unlimited/Valorie Hodgson (bottom
right); Page11: Michael Malyszko/FPG International LLC (left), International Stock/Bill Tucker
(right); Page 12: Photo Network/Esbin-Anderson (left), Photo Network/Eric Berndt (right); Page 13:
Unicorn Stock Photos/Steve Bourgeois (top), Leslie O'Shaughnessy (bottom); Page 14: (clockwise
from top left) Unicorn Stock Photos/Eric Berndt, Visuals Unlimited/Robert Clay, James Shaffer
Photography/James L. Shaffer, Telegraph Colour Library/FPG International LLC, Arthur Tilley/FPG
International LLC; Page 15: International Stock/Bill Tucker; Page 16: International Stock/Bill Tucker
(top), Unicorn Stock Photos/Jeff Greenberg (bottom left), Index Stock Imagery (bottom right)

Images used on page 3 were obtained from IMSI's MasterClips Collection, 1895 Francisco Boulevard
East, San Rafael, CA 94901-5506, USA

1 2 3 4 5 6 06 05 04 03 02 01

food for Thought

By Lisa Trumbauer

Consulting Editor: Gail Saunders-Smith, Ph.D.
Consultants: Claudine Jellison, Patricia Williams;
Reading Recovery Teachers
Content Consultant: Diana Dugan, Nursing Instructor and Campus Tutor
PIMA Medical Institute

Yellow Umbrella Books

an imprint of Capstone Press
Mankato, Minnesota

Some foods are good for you.
Some foods just taste good!

How do you know
which foods to eat?
Let's look at the food pyramid.

THE FOOD PYRAMID

LEVEL 1
Fats, Oils,
and Sweets
Group

LEVEL 2
Milk, Yogurt,
and Cheese
Group

LEVEL 3
Meat, Poultry, Fish,
Dry Beans, Eggs,
and Nuts Group

LEVEL 4
Vegetable
Group

LEVEL 5
Fruit
Group

LEVEL 6
Bread, Cereal, Rice, and Pasta Group

We can eat a little of the foods
at the top of the food pyramid.
We can eat more of the
foods at the bottom of
the food pyramid.

3

Candy and cookies have sugar.
Candy, cookies, and chips
have fat. We can eat
a little of these foods.

Just a little sugar
and fat give us energy.
But too much sugar and fat
are not good for us.

Milk, yogurt, and cheese
are dairy foods.

Dairy foods
make our
bones strong.

We can eat a little more dairy
foods than foods in Level 1.

Chicken, beef, fish, and eggs
are full of protein.
So are nuts and beans.

Protein helps us grow.
It also helps us build muscle.

Carrots, corn, and peas
are vegetables.
Apples, oranges, and bananas
are fruits.

Fruits and vegetables help to
keep us healthy. We can eat
more fruits and vegetables
than foods in Levels 1, 2, and 3.

This is the grain group.
This level includes breads,
pasta, rice, and cereal.

Grains give us energy that we can store to use later.

We can eat the most of foods in Level 6.

Which levels of the food pyramid
are shown in these pictures?

Eating good food gives us
energy, keeps us healthy,
and helps us grow.
Eating good food tastes good!

Think about the food you eat. Think about what you can eat a little of…

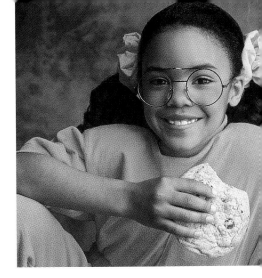

and what you can eat a lot of.

That's food for thought!

Words to Know/Index

dairy foods—foods that are made from milk; dairy foods include yogurt and cheese; page 6, 7

energy—the strength to be active without becoming tired; pages 5, 13

food pyramid—a triangle split into six areas to show the different foods people need to eat to stay healthy; people need more food from the bottom of the food pyramid than from the top; pages 2, 3, 14

fruit—the fleshy, juicy part of a plant that people eat; most fruits have seeds; pages 10, 11

grain—the seed of a cereal plant such as wheat, rice, corn, rye, or barley; pages 12, 13

level—the height or rank of something; pages 3, 4, 6, 7, 8, 10, 11, 12, 13, 14

protein—a substance found in all plants and animals; meat, eggs, beans, and fish are good sources of protein; pages 8, 9

vegetable—a part of some plants that people eat; pages 3, 10, 11

yogurt—a thick, creamy food that is made from milk; pages 3, 6

Word Count: 257
Early-Intervention Levels: 13–16